Something to Say

poems by

Erin Zinzilieta-Pennington

Finishing Line Press
Georgetown, Kentucky

Something to Say

Copyright © 2019 by Erin Zinzilieta-Pennington
ISBN 978-1-63534-884-2 First Edition
All rights reserved under International and Pan-American Copyright Conventions.
No part of this book may be reproduced in any manner whatsoever without written permission from the publisher, except in the case of brief quotations embodied in critical articles and reviews.

ACKNOWLEDGMENTS

The Sickness, *www.gemini-magazine.com*, 2018
Single Mom Waits, Blue Collar Man, Life, Cancer, Big Muddy Girl, Over,
    New Scriptor Journal, Adlai E. Stevenson High School, Lincolnshire,
    Illinois, 2009, 2010, 2013, 2015
Speak Your Language, *www.languageandculture.net*, 2008
Over, *www.midwestpoetryreview.com*, 2002
Derailment, published by Word Shop Publications, 2002
House Guest, anthology *Nature's Echo*, www.poetry.com, 2001
House Guest anthology *Treasured Poems of America*,
    www.sparrowgrasspoetryforum.com, 2000
Pen and Ink, published by The Young Writer's Guild of West Virginia, 1991
Summer at Grandma's Home (3rd place), published by *The Shagbark Review*,
    Murray State University, Murray, Kentucky, 1988

Publisher: Leah Maines
Editor: Christen Kincaid
Cover Art and Design: Eli L. Frashier
Author Photo: Erin Zinzilieta-Pennington

Printed in the USA on acid-free paper.
Order online: www.finishinglinepress.com
    also available on amazon.com

Author inquiries and mail orders:
Finishing Line Press
P. O. Box 1626
Georgetown, Kentucky 40324
U. S. A.

Table of Contents

The Stroke 1
Single Mom Waits 2
Blue Collar Man 3
Life 4
Speak Your Language 5
Geometry 6
Derailment 7
Over 8
Big Muddy Girl 9
Heaven on Earth 10
Coal Miner 11
4 p.m. 12
Peel My Love 13
Cancer 14
The Sickness 15
House Guest 16
Brief Thought 17
Love's Loom 18
Ecstasy 19
Persian Rug 20
Pen and Ink 21
Labor of Love 22
Pawn Shop Divorce 23
Behind A Picture Frame 24
Lost 25
Words 26
Wrong 27
Who Would Be My Dad? 28
Summer at Grandma's Home 29

This book is dedicated to my Father,
Dr. Joseph Zinzilieta
(July 1, 1932- September 14, 2016)

The Stroke

The coffee held up his spoon
Brown and dense like gravy
thickened by a powder
meant to keep him from choking.
He watches the clock…
hours and minutes go by
as his mind keeps ticking.
According to him it is 1964,
A year after Kennedy was assassinated.
His right arm is incapacitated,
lying limp against the bed rail
waiting for therapy.
His mind is racing…
thinking about his dog
running along the drive
following the ambulance
to the end of the road.
When can he go home?
He asks the crucifix
above the hospital door.
Nothing is like before.
The game plan has changed.
He watches from his bed,
as Molina takes the plate.
He's hoping the Cardinals hit a home run
knocking it out of the park into the street,
                      where people can still walk freely.

Single Mom

A single Mom waits
for the bills to stop
so she can buy a new coat.
    She waits for a taxi, waits for a man,
    waits for the words in her throat.
A single Mom waits for the tears to stop,
the ones that never leave.
Alone in her chair, quiet at night,
Silently she grieves.
    A single Mom waits
    for things to get better
    for the wolf to leave her door.
But the tax man cometh, leaving her empty,
always wanting more.
    A single Mom holds on
    white knuckled and nervous,
    tightening her grip on life.
Yet all this waiting, all this crying,
only ends in strife.
    A single Mom sings
    to a baby she rocks
    on her lap at night.
Hush now baby, Mockingbird baby,
Everything's going to be all right.
    She does what she does,
    all she knows how to do…
    is get down on her knees to pray.
Joy cometh in the morning…
the dawn is breaking,
as she starts a single Mom's day.

Blue Collar Man

Crevices in your face,
calluses on your hands,
Can't break down
an honest man.
Gray in your hair,
Sun in your eyes,
Can't give way
to your thin disguise.
Pretending this is what you want,
when it's all that you knew.
Metal bucket in hand,
shirt that is blue.
All that you know
is all that you live.
All that you have
is all that you give.
You'll get up tomorrow
do it again.
Pretending all the while,
time is your friend.
You know no boundaries,
know no stop.
Keep on working
with all that you've got,
blue collar man.

Life

Can't find our way to serenity,
but know the path to a bar.
Don't know why we are here
just know…that we are.

Don't have any answers,
just questions left unasked.
Too busy making a living
to get back on track.

Lost within ourselves
a time warp of years.
Our exterior is softened
by the tracks of our tears.

We go on living
half dead and half alive.
Giving all we've got
trying to survive.

They say that life is a race,
but who really wins?
When you're dying to survive,
and quitting to begin.

Speak Your Language
    ~for Raul

Speak your language to me.
Share the rich intonations of your life.
Roll your "R's",
drop your vowels,
find your ancestors in me.
Bury me in the rubble
of what use to be.
Speak to me in your language,
describing all things
masculine and feminine
from the beginning.

Geometry

The geometry of you and I,
Lies somewhere
in the X and Y.
We are two variables,
yet one whole.

Derailment

Memories of you escape me
like a train traveling too fast.
Feeling the vibrations of the ground
beneath my feet,
you rattle my world.
Hearing your voice in my head
is like a train whistle
slicing through the air at midnight.
Next, I see you fading away
into the distance.
It is just a matter of time
before I am
        d
           e
              r
                 ailed.

Over

You once asked me if we were over.
What is over?
a preposition describing direction
No, that answer would not satisfy your panic.
How do I know if we are over?
I never knew we were under…
Under the gun you are holding at my head.
No. We are not over.
Not even as I find amusement in your panic.

Big Muddy Girl

As a child I walked
in the wide-eyed haze of youth,
along the banks of the Big Muddy River,
with a cattail between my teeth
and mud between my toes.
I hid in the shadows of oaks,
lingering along the shore,
counting dragonflies in the sun
dreaming of my life in years to come.
Oblivious to the fact,
it couldn't get much better than this,
walking along the Big Muddy River
in cut-off jeans.

Heaven on Earth

Heaven must be cornfields furrowed in the spring
and lilac bushes in full bloom.

Heaven must be honeysuckle in a young girl's hair,
too busy kissing her young man to brush the petals free.

Heaven must be sunshine warming your face,
tanning your shoulders as you sleep in the grass.

Heaven must be the first falling star you've ever seen
while lying in the arms of someone you love.

Heaven must be skinny-dipping in cool pond water,
allowing it to skim your body like silk.

Heaven must be… like June in the Midwest.

Coal Miner

Today I saw a coal miner
trying to hold on to life with both hands.
It was slipping away,
with his absence of sleep
lack of peace.
Crevices in his face,
eyes sunk back in his head,
all confirmed, the earth owned him.

4 p.m.

One single ray of light,
falling in a dusty mote
upon a cornstalk at four in the afternoon,
standing in a gilded world
awakening the soul and spirit,
reminding us …
                    nothing is by chance.

Peel My Love

Peel my love like an onion,
layer upon layer uncover me.
Get to the core,
to the root of my desires.
Try to understand me,
where I am coming from,
going to, don't want to be.
Peel my love like an onion,
loving the fragments
that make up the whole
                    of me.

Cancer

Cancer Ward, Suite B
lime green walls greet me.
I am 38 years old
and in perfect health.
Who knew?
I'm inexperienced,
I don't know how to be sick.
Maybe I should have been interviewed
so I could play the part?
I have a cough, big deal.
Okay, I've had it four months.
I can't have cancer!
Cancer is not me.
Like tattoos and cheap perfume
It is not something I would *do*.
People stare. My Dad totters behind me.
They probably think he is sick.
After all, he is 76.
Nope, it's me,
The 38 year old full of tumors,
Hanging out in the Cancer Ward, Suite B,
waiting.

The Sickness

Waited for a call
that never came.
Waited for a bell
that never rang.
Waited for a love
that would endure.
Had the sickness
but felt no cure.
Waited for someone
to stick around.
Always lost,
but never found.

House Guest

Two years ago
I was your lover
coming and going
as I pleased
having my own key.

Today I am a guest, a visitor,
knocking before entering.

To think I walked these halls
wearing only revelry.
Whatever was I thinking?

Estranged to it all
I leave…
        grasping for the doorknob
        in the dark.

Brief Thought

Life comes to me in slow steady drips,
like a leaky faucet with no hope of being fixed.
Each and every drop adds to my existence,
—as my cup runneth over.

Love's Loom

Can you weave me into the tapestry of your life?
combining the reds and indigoes and so on
Can you bind our lives together?
over and under into one
Can you hold me as a loom holds yarn?
tautly and securely
Can you weave me into the tapestry of your life?
without fraying the ends

Ecstasy

Wrap me in angelic wings
unknown to mortal men.
Carry me away from earth
and set me down again.
Caress my every whisper.
Fill my every need.
Entrap me in your love,
yet set my spirit free.

Persian Rug

Carpeting space within my mind
entangling thoughts in color,
lost in a maze of zigzags and fringe.
Is love red on black? Or black on red?
Hiding among ecru boundaries,
waiting for someone to save me,
or interrupt my thoughts with a vacuum.

Pen and Ink
> ~*For Debbie Hellerstein*

"Let the pen be an extension of your hand…"

Controlled fluid lines
flow carefully
across the canvas
permeating the pores
of white cotton.

Bringing to life
her essence.

Filling up
the negative space
in his world.

Crosshatching
the darks and lights of love,
a vehicle of his desires.

Extending the bounds
of imagination.

Suddenly,
she is alive.

Living in the eyes
of his audience,
and in the shadows
of pen and ink.

Labor of Love

Pressing a quilt block
getting the seams straight,
mind racing back
to another day.
           Remembering…
           ironing your shirts.
           How I loved you to look
           nice and neat.
Trying desperately to be
your model wife.
Starching your collar,
creasing the sleeves,
smoothing the placket
so buttons would lie flat.
Each stripe was so crisp
standing at attention,
every crease was perfection,
no buttonhole went unnoticed.
           Humming to myself today,
           I remember loving you
           so intensely back then.
Living only for you
and our daughter,
and a closet full
of pinstriped shirts,
each a labor of love.

Pawn Shop Divorce

In a glass case
are boxes of rings.

Yours and mine
and theirs in between.

Divided by rows
of broken vows.

Trays and trays
of then and now.

Only eighty-eight dollars
for a band of gold.

And all the happiness
a lifetime can hold.

The man behind the counter
with golden teeth
offers me twelve bucks
and a sigh of relief.

He grants me permission
to live my life.
As he takes away the burden
of being your wife.

Behind a Picture Frame

Happy faces look out at me,
from behind a picture frame.

Me and you
and you and me,
once together, now apart.

She and you
and you and she,
and me . . .
with a broken heart.

We were smiling
then crying.
Now I am dying
from behind a picture frame.

Lost

Based on "The World Is Too Much With Us"
by William Wordsworth

I am too much in this world
as my wax wings melt
dripping into this abyss,
we call life.
I am too much in this hell
we call love,
to understand what is true love,
and what is not.
I am too much in this moment
to consider the past, or future,
as the present, swallows me whole.
I am too much into you
To know what is me,
or us, or so on.
I am too much in this world,
as my tears become tidal waves.

Words

Bitter words you speak
descend upon my body
like silent raindrops
running down an oiled pane.
Leaving behind
a shiny, slimy trail,
attesting to their having been.

Wrong

If I asked you to come back
it would be for all the wrong reasons,
the hour, the drive, the weather, the season.
If I asked you to come back
it would be wrong.

Who Would Be My Dad?

Who would get up to make coffee?
Rattling pots and pans, waking the dead,
measuring grains spilling most on the counter.
Who would feed your beagles?
All six, running the pen from end to end,
waiting for you in your flannel shirt to feed them.
Who would wake me in the morning?
Flicking on the bedroom light
calling out, "Sissy it's time to get up!"
in that annoying, I'm a morning person voice.
Who would occupy the bathroom?
Steaming up the mirror,
leaving beard stubble in the sink and Aramis in the air.
Who would go to town in your orange hunting hat?
All year 'round looking ridiculous.
Who would give "Red" the town hanger 'round,
a buck or two for coffee
without questioning the beer on his breath?
Who would come home to Mom, John, Scott, and me?
Fall asleep at the dinner table then deny the whole incident.
Who would plant a garden?
Putting out enough tomatoes and cucumbers for all of Benton.
Who would feed the cardinals, kill the blackbirds, and prune the fruit trees?
Who would Mom and I pick up after?
A sock here and suspenders there.
Who would tell us all good-night?
Locking the doors,
closing the windows,
keeping us safe.
Who would be my Dad?

Summer at Grandma's Home

Sunday at Grandma's
were the most important thing in my life.
First, we would go to church,
then go to Grandma's at 12:00 sharp.
You could smell the pasta through the screen door
and all the neighbors would rave!
After lunch, we had the rest of the day to play.
Jumping rope in perfect time...
      Swish,
       Swish,
        Swish...
Playing kickball with the redbud bush as second base...
When we grew tired
Grandma would get out her old purple bedspread
and we'd lay under a shaded oak tree.
At dusk, all the grownups would sit outside
in lawn chairs or the old swing...
      Gossiping,
       Gossiping,
        Snapping beans...
Sometimes, Dad would even make homemade ice cream,
And we would eat as the mosquitoes devoured us.
But the most fun came when it grew dark...
We would all play "ghost in the graveyard".
Uncle Jim was always the ghost.
"Ghost in the graveyard!" we would all call,
Holding hands as we ran across the yard—
followed by street lamp shadows.
Soon it would be time to go home
As we kissed Grandma good-bye,
She would say, "All I can see are the whites of your eyes!"
We would run off laughing,
as our tired bodies jumped one last time for fireflies.
The smell of lilac bushes and the croaking of frogs
would then send three tired grandkids fast to sleep...
        Dreaming of Grandma's home.

Ms. Erin Zinzilieta-Pennington is a 2010 graduate of McKendree University where she earned a Master's Degree in Educational Leadership. She is also a 1994 graduate of Eastern Illinois University having attained a B.A. in Secondary Education English. Ms. Pennington began her college career at Rend Lake Junior College having graduated with an A.A. in Education. She is a 1988 graduate of Benton Consolidated High School. Ms. Pennington has been an educator since 1994. She has been teaching at Carmi-White County High School since August of 2000. She was a part-time instructor of English at Rend Lake Junior College (1994-1998) and Southeastern Illinois Junior College (2002-2003). Pennington has been a part-time weekly opinion columnist for *The Carmi Times* since 2012. Her poetry has appeared in *New Scriptor*, a book forum, for and by educators, produced by Adlai E. Stevenson High School, Lincolnshire, Illinois. Ms. Pennington was a featured writer in *New Scriptor* in 2009, 2010, 2013 and 2015. Pennington's work has also appeared in online journals such as www.geminimagazine.com, www.languageandculture.net, www.midwestpoetryreview.com. Ms. Pennington currently resides in Carmi, Illinois, where she is within driving distance of her daughter, son-in-law, and grandchildren.

www.ingramcontent.com/pod-product-compliance
Lightning Source LLC
LaVergne TN
LVHW041508070426
835507LV00012B/1421